The Weight of Shadows

poems by

Corey D. Cook

Finishing Line Press
Georgetown, Kentucky

The Weight of Shadows

ISBN 978-1-63534-830-9 First Edition

ACKNOWLEDGMENTS

Grateful acknowledgment is made to the editors of the following
publications in which these pieces first appeared (some in earlier versions
and some under different titles).

Dreams: *Pearl*
The Spring of Our Freshman Year of High School: *Willard & Maple*
Long Sands Beach (York, Maine): *Freshwater*
One-Year-Old Hands: *Wild Goose Poetry Review*
Inpatient: *Rat's Ass Review*
The Night My Cousin Shot Himself: *East Coast Literary Review*
Prognosis: *Dime Show Review*
stillborn: *Down in the Dirt*
Searching for Jane Kenyon: *Northern New England Review*
for the friend that helped me with my spelling in school: *Rusty Truck*
Waiting: *The Pangolin Review*
Iris: *After the Pause*
My Cousin's TV: *Melancholy Hyperbole*
July 4th: *Muddy River Poetry Review*
reading: *Yellow Chair Review*
Nana's Last Boat Ride: *Freshwater*
At the Donald Hall Reading in Woodstock, Vermont on July 27, 2013:
Dewpoint Literary Journal

Publisher: Leah Maines
Editor: Christen Kincaid
Cover Art: Rachael D. Cook
Author Photo: Rachael D. Cook
Cover Design: Leah Huete

Printed in the USA on acid-free paper.
Order online: www.finishinglinepress.com
             also available on amazon.com

Author inquiries and mail orders:
Finishing Line Press
P. O. Box 1626
Georgetown, Kentucky 40324
U. S. A.

Table of Contents

Dreams

for Roddy

Dreams

"I want to know...that dreams are not my home..."
—Rosanne Cash

Those picture shows I don't pay for
but see over and over and over again, those
picture shows that are projected, projected
in a dark theater, a theater thought

to be closed for the night. Those picture
shows that star me as the hunted, hunted
by Donkey-Kong, Donkey-Kong the computer-
generated gorilla, the gorilla that throws

barrels at me as I try to outrun him. Hunted
by an unidentified man with piercing eyes, eyes
that peer through my windows, windows that
he shatters with his gloved hand, his gloved hand

that grabs at me as I climb stairs and slam
doors. Those picture shows I hope to forget
as soon as I pass below the EXIT and make
my way home, home that is anywhere but here.

"Let us praise death that raises itself to such power that nothing but death exists."

—*Donald Hall*

The Spring of Our Freshman Year of High School

Our class trickled through the double doors of the school and pooled in a wooded area to play capture the flag. After the teacher chose teams, explained rules and defined boundaries, a friend and her male companion scaled a mossy embankment and had sex behind a stirring curtain of sapling buds.

A month later she found me in study hall and mouthed *I think I'm pregnant.* Reluctantly, my older cousin agreed to drive me to the CVS several towns away after school so I could buy a pregnancy test. The next day I offered her the bag and a quick hug behind the baseball dugout between classes.

That same week I snuck out of the house and met up with you at the structure on the elementary school's lower playground. Our spot. We huddled together on the pea stone and you asked me if I was ready as I stared up at the stars—thousands of glaring plus signs.

Long Sands Beach (York, Maine)

We sit on the cement stairs
and watch a seagull poke
a rumpled paper bag
with its beak
as the tide comes in

You tell me your mother
was prone to fits of rage
Destroyed so many things
Not a single heirloom spared
   Depression glass
   Hand-woven baskets
   Stoneware jugs

I ask if she was ever physical
with you and you turn away
Stare at the relentless waves

Waves that reach out
for the broken
For the discarded
   Shards of glass
   Splintered sticks
   Crushed stones

Waves that will soften
their sharp edges
Their pointy tips

Transform them into
things to hold on to
Things to cherish

One-Year-Old Hands

> *"[She] cannot stop taking the hands from room to room, learning*
> *the names of everything [she] wants."*
> —*Wesley McNair*

Hands that swipe day old spaghetti from the trashcan, pull
fistfuls of fur from the cat's broad back. Hands that dump

boxes of crackers on the kitchen floor, leave smear marks
on doors and windows. Hands that take a carton of heavy

cream from grocery bag to the "cupboard" under the living
room chair, fiddle with the knobs on the stove. Hands that rip

pages from the $75.00 book of photographs on the coffee table,
swat at siblings intent on taking toys away. Hands we coax away

from wanting with sing song voices, guide away with curled
fingers, distract from wanting with smiling faces and puckered lips.

Assault on a Marriage #1

Giving birth to a baby
with no breath sounds
No pulse

Assault on a Marriage #2

Being transferred from the maternity ward
to the psychiatric ward
after giving birth to a baby
with no breath sounds
No pulse

Inpatient

The trees outside the window
are as familiar to me now

as the lean and weathered figures
in the black and white photo

on my roommate's crowded hospital tray.
Her father, mother, uncles and aunts

in the summer of 1927.
Immigrants new to the country.

Posing on a grassy knoll.
Hands behind their backs.

The sun high above them.
Shadows just starting to take root.

The Night My Cousin Shot Himself

The meteorologist had remarked
on the clear skies
during the 5:00 o'clock news.

A star gazing kind of night.

And I couldn't help but see
the constellation above
my cousin's head
as I drove to his house
after mom's frantic call.

Blood spatter against
an unfinished pine headboard.

Each spot rounded
and still reflecting light.

Assault on a Marriage #3

Persistent abdominal pain
which leads to a MRI
which leads to "suspicious" lesions

Prognosis

There are moments when I forget
about the lesions in my abdomen.

And then I notice a Mason jar
filled with polished black stones.

A telephone pole
peppered with nail heads

A field rife with Brown-eyed Susans.
Their centers cone-shaped.
Protruding.

Or your nostrils as you stand over me
reading treatment options aloud.

Though I only hear the pauses in between sentences.
Only see the periods scattered across the page.

stillborn

the grief counselor
walked us to our car

we thanked her

pulled onto pleasant street

minutes after the bell rang
at the local elementary school

seconds after the buses filled

so many small faces
in the windows

including a boy
who reminded us
of the baby we buried

dark unruly hair
broad nose
chubby cheeks

who smiled warmly
waved enthusiastically

forced us to say goodbye again

Searching for Jane Kenyon

*"She recedes into the granite museum of JANE KENYON
1947-1995."*

—Donald Hall

I pull the car onto the shoulder of Route 4,
under the shade of a red maple,
sit and stare at the graveyard,
the sloping hill,
headstones,
their long shadows

Wonder which one is hers,
if she picked it out herself,
or if that unfortunate job was left
to her grief-stricken husband,
who filled books with poems about her illness,
her death

Wish I could tell her that "Having it Out
with Melancholy" has been a lifeline for me,
reminds me that I am not the only one
that draws the curtains on sunny days,
ignores the telephone,
lets it cry and cry in its black cradle,
goes without groceries,
unable to walk into the general store,
to face the cashier,
the good-natured banter of the regulars

I decide I am not ready to say goodbye,
for the finality of it all,
stay in the car,
feel for the tablet of Xanax,
a lump in the throat of my pocket

At home another drug to try,
one that just might reacquaint me
with the "talk" button on my phone,
the store,
its warped wooden floors,
narrow aisles,
dust-covered cans,
the cashier who will call me by my name,
will ask where I've been

for the friend that helped me with my spelling in school

your mugshot
made the 11 o'clock news

pulled over for talking
on your cell phone
arrested after they found cocaine
and drug paraphernalia in your car

face still youthful
hair tucked neatly behind your ears
lips pursed
eyes dark and distant
like the silhouettes
of a mother and father
walking away
from their child

you sat right behind me in school
blonde hair teased
clad in umbros regardless
of the season

helped me spell hundreds
and hundreds of words

words like *recovery*
stability
maybe even *prosperity*

Waiting

In the weeks I waited
for the biopsy results
I had the same recurring dream

Standing at the French door
Panic-stricken
as a hulking black bear
paced the lawn
Pugnacious and unfazed
by my attempts
to spook him

He wouldn't leave
Kept scavenging for food
Stripping berry bushes
Digging up bulbs
with paws the size
of snow shovels

Eventually I worked up
the nerve to reach
for the knob
Pull open the door
Only to find myself awake

Lying in bed

The scar still there
The threat still close

Iris

The vet said it was cancer.
That it would only be a matter of time.

And, naively, we thought she would wait
for death stretched out in a sun patch.
Or curled up in the wicker basket
on top of the refrigerator.
A halogen bulb burning brightly above her.

But she went looking for it instead.
In the hulking shadows of chairs.
Behind the potted houseplants.
Under the black belt of the treadmill.
In the dim alleyway between the washer and dryer.
Beside the stacked soup cans in the pantry.

Finally found it in the smallest room of the dollhouse.
In the only room without a window.
Primitive birds on the wall paper.
Acrylic flames in the fireplace—
unmoved and cold to the touch.

My Cousin's TV

was left on our doorstep
a month after his funeral
with a note taped
to the back.

He wanted you to have this.

The TV that is now centered
on an antique dresser
in our living room.

And no matter what channel
we watch, the only thing
I see is his reflection
in the screen the day
he killed himself.

Sitting on the edge
of his bed.
Hair a dark cloud above
his downturned face.
Gun in his left hand.
Yellow legal pad
on the nightstand.

Sitting there smoldering
like the cigarette
in the ashtray
beside him.

Before he lays back
with the barrel
in his mouth.
Finger on the trigger.

July 4th

You tell me you are leaving
for good this time

Pull each car seat
from the back
of your sedan

Line them up
by the stone wall

Toss your house key
onto the bristly
welcome mat

Drive away slowly
as our kids hang
from the monkey bars
like solemn flags

The Wheel of Fortune Puzzle That Haunts Me

BOUNC_NG B_BY BOY

reading

the day after the doctor called with the biopsy results
i sat with an open book in my lap to discourage questions
uneasy conversations

sat and thought about the larvae of the lily leaf beetle
i found in my garden the week before

thought about their slug-like bodies
so small and so many
the mounds of brown excrement on their backs
those grotesque landscapes

thought about the missing foliage
buds

wondered what would be taken next

Nana's Last Boat Ride

We planned to show her
the wild blueberry bushes
on Oliver Island,
the freshly painted door
of her favorite cottage,
the loons' nest
on the muddy embankment,

but she was not able
to hold her head up,
the latest side effect
of Alzheimer's,

so she stared at the floor
of the boat,
the rusty anchor,
the coiled nylon rope,
the shadows cast
by her children,
her grandchildren,

shadows so indistinct
they could only belong
to strangers.

At the Donald Hall Reading in Woodstock, Vermont
on July 27, 2013

He sits and reads on the stage. Lucid and witty. Walker idle
beside him. Hair disheveled. Sunken neck obscured by grey
beard. He reads a poem about Jane. His wife. Who had it out

with leukemia. And lost. Donald clears his throat. Another
poem about their dog, Gus. And the couple sitting in front

of me face each other. Mouths downturned. Eyes watery
and reflective. Clutching each others' hands. A green onyx
ring on her index finger. More hazel than green. Like your

eyes. Those wide and welcoming orbs. Framed by thick brown
hair. Each one anchored by a scattering of faint freckles. The

only constellations I have mapped with my fingertips. I know
that you and I would have looked at each other in the same way.
Donald clears his throat. And I am *alone again with [your] absence.*

~ *The quote in italics appears in "The After Life" by Donald Hall*

Corey D. Cook is the author of four other poetry collections: *Rhododendron in a Time of War* (Scars Publications), *What to Do with a Dying Parakeet* (Pudding House Publications), *Flock* (Origami Poems Project) and *White Flag Raised* (Kattywompus Press). His work has appeared in *the Aurorean, Ballard Street Poetry Journal, Brevities, Chiron Review, Columbia College Literary Review, Dewpoint Literary Journal, East Coast Literary Review, Entelechy International, Freshwater, Loch Raven Review, Lummox, Muddy River Poetry Review, Northern New England Review, Pearl,* and *The Somerville News*. Corey edited *The Orange Room Review* with his wife, Rachael, for eight years (2006-2014) and currently edits *Red Eft Review*. He works at a hospital in New Hampshire and lives in Vermont.

www.ingramcontent.com/pod-product-compliance
Lightning Source LLC
LaVergne TN
LVHW021125080426
835510LV00021B/3320